I Made
A Place
For You

I Made
A Place
For You

Damian White

atmosphere press

Contents

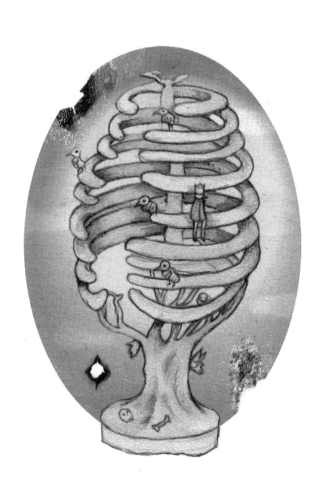

Post Mortem

We abracadabra our flaws
into a mausoleum of deceit

For a semblance of redemption
in shelling our leprosy inside

I always loved the ones we bury
our uncanny trove of white lies

When I expire, inscribe my epitaph
on Pandora's decaying box

Hum melodiously as you adorn
my headstone with pastel foliage

Let it read:

"Here lies a man who
never died inside."

Morning Glow

Trees cascade in stale winds
a new day looms

Time ebbs faithfully
with the synchronicity of firefly tails

My praying hands tremble
feebly at time's holy
alchemy:

Lord, thank you for excavating my flaws
allowing me to breathe

Amen.

Wolf on a Cliff

I'm
beginning
to believe again

I've clawed up abyssal valleys
to learn a plateau is a peak draped in

sheep's clothing and perhaps life's finest vantage point

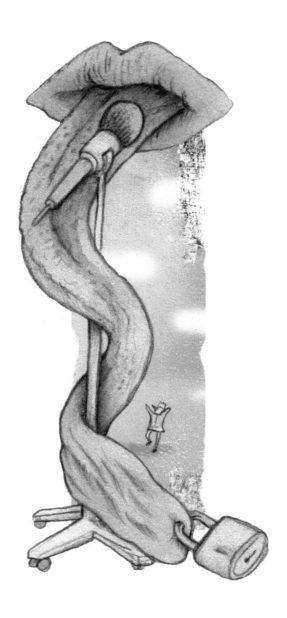

God's Typewriter

The Golden Rule of speech is
to speak when spoken through

Be a prophet of God's whispers
sacral thoughts
resurrect the spine
unveil the stature of man
and poise his pen

Am I the poem or poet?
words linger on my tongue
forlorn and ephemeral

I am more written than writer
an opus of cathartic scribble
unfurling my fleshiest truth

Sacred Math

If death is imminent
chalk it up to gravity's incessant
desire to bloody its ivory tusks

Don't blame beasts of burden
death's talons assail
according to God's plan

Who am I to rework His math?
each abacus bead shifted
is intentional

We are integral.

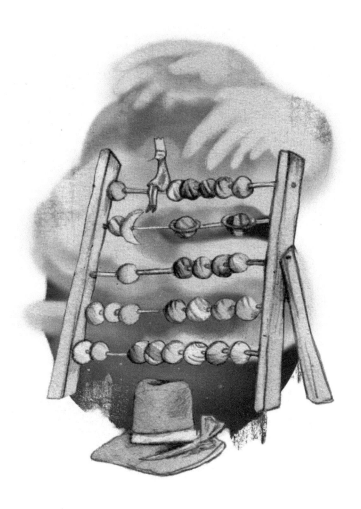

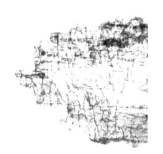

Pinky Promise

You broke

        pinky promises

                for a life of absence

of enmity

        running down

              stained skin

I did what sons do

          tried to forgive

               the bigger
               person

Growth Spurt

I
Prayed
On
Teary Pillows
For You
To Exorcise
The Child
In Me

Quiet
His Relentless
Torment
And
Let
Me Be
Man

Peacefully

We Locked Eyes

I'm the apogee of my untruths
a burial ground of missteps
once fertile, yet fashioned futile
an elegy of dormant desires

I've made a mockery of mirrors
stood coyly in center frame
deflected in fragility and
grimaced at my reflection

It's the spirit of a man
that unearths his ill soul
renders him villainous
a mere scrap of himself

We locked eyes
too repulsed
to coax a smile
on the sadder days

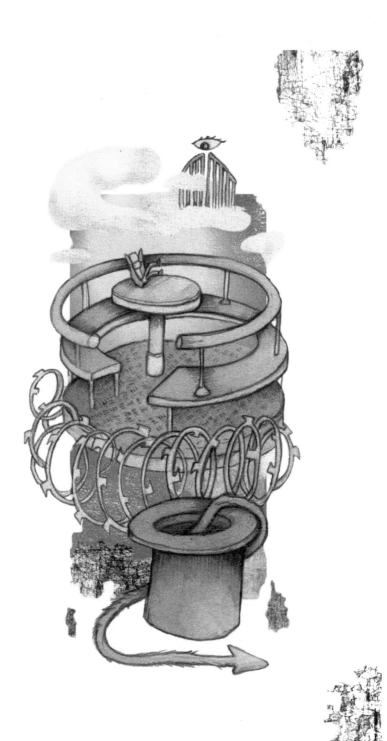

A Man Deveined

Two felonies in my pocket
one to snort, one to shoot
a perilous pair of pastimes

Beware of Nirvana
I never knew what blooms
once demons seed inward

Mother said, "an idle mind
is the devil's playground"
before the melancholy

I wield guilt's sword
unsheathed and wobbly
my wrist pours out

Look Away

I
only
regret
the moment
I promised
to never
avert
my eyes
no matter
how brutal
the
sight

I Am Innocent

To grieve is to soothe
      an abscess
Reconcile the strife
      between faith and fate
For freedom is no
      wavering white flag
We build a fortress
      of validation
           and guillotine
                our most
                    precious birthright:
                    Innocence.

We swoon between
      slithering temptation
Holiness roosting
      in the umbrage
Yet, will we emerge
      Victorious? Yes.

Heaven's doors
      open serendipitously
Ushered by God's
      palm itself
Our journey is
      the price of admission.

Pixie Dust

A word to the unwise:

Wisdom Is The Pixie Dust

Speckled On Yesterday's Memories

Sky Dweller

Stars glitz and birth
celestial lighthouses nightlong
guiding the wayward home

The sun bastions the moon
cradles her
after charioting the sky

Clouds soften the wind's
untimely falls
and revel triumphantly

I laud heavenly virtues
the noble cosmos remains
a sky dweller's refuge

Good Mourning

Are we soot?
Impure, black, and
better suited for
sadness.

Quite the contrary
if all things
be considered
impartially.

We are soil.
Basal, vital, and
better suited for
sunshine.

Devil Bait

Never dare the devil to dance
be wary of lasciviousness
as his swindling hips tango
beside Eden's chancel

Never dare the devil to sing
serpents awaken sacred chakras
reek of sinful incantation
under the charmer's murky sky

If you do, cradle your blessings
summon a soul's worth of prayers now
for no war is won in worry
dance and sing as you wish

A Sinner's Plea

A God-fearing man once said,
"Faith quells the fear of fleeting time."

Arraigned at the neck of Christ's Cross,
I ask you with clenched teeth
and palms humbly splayed

Is a weary sinner worth saving?

Balance Due

Give me more
than I can handle

I can handle more than
I give myself credit for

It's just debt's toll
pay or be payment

To whom do I
owe my soul?

Scorpion Claws

I flirted with death often
and escaped pregnant with indecency

I appraised my worth egregiously
for guiding a withering elder's hand

The libra scale tilts unfavorably
I am burden and burdened

Still, I contort
to no man's will

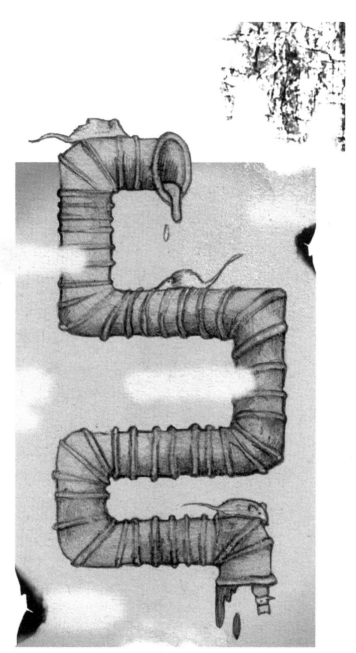

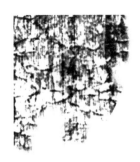

Hunger Pangs

Depression is gluttonous.
A ravenous sin
with startling gusto.

Gorging itself on our
pomp and circumstance
until revulsed.

Bad Memories

To frack any modicum of clarity
from our treachery is momentum

We abhor the glory in eluding
despair's vile grip

Rather, let us cease to revel
in old miseries so fondly

Purgatory

I am masterfully
patient these days
Liberation eclipses
the burden of waiting

Finally
unclipped at the
helm of bliss
I am still

When you return,
I will don growth rings
bowed majestically
in surrender

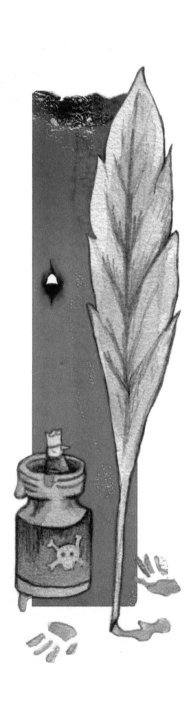

Written in Blood

As ink bleeds,
I'm a sacrificial
soul's feast

Pain gushes
exhumed from
ghastly night terrors

Words abet my
inner masochist's
bloodletting pen

As ink bleeds,
I bleed

Playing God

I gave myself God's glory
He lent it to me briefly

My shoulders buckled
beneath its magnificence

To be Godly is
not to be God.

About Atmosphere Press

Atmosphere Press is an independent, full-service publisher for excellent books in all genres and for all audiences. Learn more about what we do at atmospherepress.com.

We encourage you to check out some of Atmosphere's latest releases, which are available at Amazon.com and via order from your local bookstore:

Until the Kingdom Comes, poetry by Jeanne Lutz

Warcrimes, poetry by GOODW.Y.N

The Freedom of Lavenders, poetry by August Reynolds

Convalesce, poetry by Enne Zale

Poems for the Bee Charmer (And Other Familiar Ghosts), poetry by Jordan Lentz

Serial Love: When Happily Ever After... Isn't, poetry by Kathy Kay

Flowers That Die, poetry by Gideon Halpin

Through The Soul Into Life, poetry by Shoushan B

Embrace The Passion In A Lover's Dream, poetry by Paul Turay

Reflections in the Time of Trumpius Maximus, poetry by Mark Fishbein

Drifters, poetry by Stuart Silverman

As a Patient Thinks about the Desert, poetry by Rick Anthony Furtak

Winter Solstice, poetry by Diana Howard

Blindfolds, Bruises, and Break-Ups, poetry by Jen Schneider

Songs of Snow and Silence, poetry by Jen Emery

INHABITANT, poetry by Charles Crittenden

Godless Grace, poetry by Michael Terence O'Brien

March of the Mindless, poetry by Thomas Walrod

In the Village That Is Not Burning Down, poetry by Travis Nathan Brown

Mud Ajar, poetry by Hiram Larew

To Let Myself Go, poetry by Kimberly Olivera Lainez

I Am Not Young And I Will Die With This Car In My Garage, poetry by Blake Rong

About the Author

Damian White is a writer from Columbus, OH. He is the author of the poetry book, *I Made A Place For You*, which is his debut collection. After battling two bouts with homelessness, he channeled those experiences into poetry as a way to heal a fractured identity.

When not writing, he can be found exploring art galleries, playing tug-of-war with his pups, traveling, and finding the best coffee in every city.

Damian received his B.A. in Sociology from Davidson College. He currently resides in his hometown with his wife and stepchildren.

About the Artist

Francesco Orazzini is a visual artist and illustrator, originally from Livorno, Italy. His work has been exhibited in galleries and museums around the world, including in Italy, USA, Mexico, England, Colombia, Spain, Portugal, Germany, Africa, and Belgium.

He has produced compelling visual content for art festivals, books, magazines, newspapers, walls, theaters, clothing lines, musicians, coins, and an array of freelance projects.

Currently, he resides in Mexico City, where he leads illustration, design, and painting classes at the Faculty of Art and Design.

CPSIA information can be obtained
at www.ICGtesting.com
Printed in the USA
LVHW070826121022
730468LV00021B/600